MOUNT
Rushmore

BY LUKE GABRIEL

Published by The Child's World®
1980 Lookout Drive • Mankato, MN 56003-1705
800-599-READ • www.childsworld.com

Acknowledgments
The Child's World®: Mary Berendes, Publishing Director
The Design Lab: Design
Jody Jensen Shaffer: Editing
Red Line Editorial: Photo Research

Photo credits
PhotoDisc_USLndmks, cover; Library of Congress, 5, 13; Harris
& Ewing/Library of Congress, 6; Alfred Eisenstaedt/Time & Life
Pictures/Getty Images, 9; Creatas, 10, 18; FPG/Getty Images,
14; Frederic Lewis/Getty Images, 17; Barnes Ian/Shutterstock
Images, 21

ISBN 9781623239558
LCCN 2013947301

Printed in the United States of America
Mankato, MN
November, 2013
PA02189

ABOUT THE AUTHOR

Luke Gabriel enjoys traveling, reading, playing games with his wife, and wrestling with his five children. He and his family live in Eagan, Minnesota.

TABLE OF CONTENTS

The Monument

"Higher, higher!" This is the command of a worker carving a huge stone face. The year is 1935. The face is being carved on the top of a mountain called Mount Rushmore in western South Dakota. A giant carving called a **monument** was being created. But why was a monument being carved on the top of a South Dakota mountain? That's what many people wanted to know.

It all started in 1923. That was when a man named Doane Robinson had an idea. He thought that a huge monument should be created in South Dakota's Black Hills to mark the end of the Great Plains and the beginning of the Rocky Mountains. This monument would show how much the United States had grown over the last 150 years.

These workers are carving the face of George Washington.

Gutzon Borglum

The Sculptor

In 1867, a boy named Gutzon Borglum was born near Bear Lake, Idaho. He wanted to be an artist. His brother was an artist. When he grew up, Gutzon went to Paris to study art. The type of art he liked best was called sculpting. A **sculptor** is an artist who carves statues out of stone or other materials.

When Gutzon moved back to the United States, he started making sculptures. He carved statues for a **cathedral**, or big church, in New York City. He was chosen to carve a big statue of President Lincoln at the Capitol in Washington, D.C. In 1915, Gutzon was chosen to carve a giant sculpture on Stone Mountain in Georgia. He became known as the "Giant Sculpture Maker." Because he was such a good sculptor, Gutzon was chosen to carve the monument in the Black Hills.

Choosing the Mountain

At first, some people thought a monument should be carved in a part of the Black Hills called the Needles. The Needles were tall mountains that stood together in a row. Gutzon wandered around the Black Hills and saw a better place to build the monument. This was Mount Rushmore. The **peak** of this mountain was more than 6,000 feet (1,829 meters) high. It was made of hard rock called **granite**. It faced towards the sun most of the day.

But what type of monument should be carved? Gutzon looked at the mountain and got the idea to carve the faces of four presidents. He talked with many people but couldn't easily decide which presidents to pick. Choosing which presidents to carve was a very important decision!

Gutzon Borglum decided against using the Needles for the monument.

Choosing the four presidents was a difficult task.

Picking the Presidents

The mountain could fit four faces, and Gutzon wanted to pick the four presidents who most helped the United States to grow. He chose George Washington and decided to put him at the highest and most important spot on the mountain. That was because Washington was our first president and led the United States in the Revolutionary War.

Next, Gutzon chose President Thomas Jefferson. Jefferson wrote the Declaration of Independence and helped our country expand west. Gutzon then chose Presidents Theodore Roosevelt and Abraham Lincoln. Roosevelt built the Panama Canal and was known as a great adventurer. Lincoln wrote the **Emancipation Proclamation** and guided our country through the Civil War.

Preparing to Carve

The first step was to make a small **model** of the monument. This model would contain small sculptures of the presidents' heads and faces. Borglum also drew **sketches** of what the monument should look like. He used photographs and paintings to help create the faces. He made small sculptures of each president out of plaster. But how would he make sure the big monument would match the model?

Gutzon invented a measuring tool to measure the model exactly. He measured the noses, ears, eyes, and other features of each face. Gutzon then placed a giant measuring tool on top of Mount Rushmore. He used this tool to mark the exact location of each part of the mountain to be carved. Gutzon and other workers hung from ropes and put marks on the mountain. When Mount Rushmore was all marked, Gutzon and his crew could start the carving!

*Borglum created this smaller sculpture to get an
idea of how the monument would look.*

Dynamite had to be used to prepare Mount Rushmore for the monument.

Blasting Rock

The first step of carving the monument was to remove large chunks of rock from the side of the mountain. Usually people used explosives called **dynamite** to break up rock. Gutzon didn't want to use dynamite because he thought it might destroy the mountain. He tried other ways to break up the rock, but the granite was too hard. He decided he had to use dynamite.

Workers drilled holes into the side of the mountain. Then they put dynamite into the holes and blasted out big chunks of rock. They measured carefully, because they didn't want to make any mistakes. They were able to use Gutzon's measuring tool to know exactly where to drill the holes and put the dynamite.

Carving the Mountain

Once the big chunks of granite were removed, the actual carving of the faces began. Workers hung from the mountain on ropes and used both hand tools and power tools. They used power drills to drill lots of holes close together. Then they used hammers and chisels to chisel off the rock. Because the granite was so hard, the tools got dull very fast. Every day the tools had to be sharpened. When all the drilling, chiseling, and carving were done, Gutzon inspected the faces. He told the workers to smooth over any rough spots. They used air-powered hammers to do this. When the smoothing was finished, the polished granite looked white.

These workers are carving Abraham Lincoln's face into the granite.

The heads on Mount Rushmore are 60 feet (18 meters) tall.
They can be seen from 60 miles (about 97 kilometers) away.

The Finished Monument

It took only seven years to carve the faces, but it took 14 years for the monument to be completely finished. Gutzon spent most of his time planning and raising money to pay for it. It cost $1 million, which was hard to raise because the country was going through the **Great Depression**. It was a very difficult time for our country, and there wasn't much extra money to give to a project like this. Gutzon went to the U.S. Congress and convinced the government to pay for most of the project.

Gutzon himself didn't live to see the final monument. He died in March of 1941. His son, Lincoln Borglum, took over and finished the monument for his father. It was finished on October 31, 1941.

Visiting Mount Rushmore

Mount Rushmore has a **studio** or small museum that has Gutzon's sculptures, drawings, and tools used to carve the monument. There is a park called the Avenue of Flags at the base of the monument. The park has the flags of all 50 states plus the U.S. territories. Visitors can walk along the Avenue of Flags and then go to trails that head up the mountain.

The area around Mount Rushmore is a national park. It is a beautiful area with streams, trees, and wild animals. About 3 million people visit every year. If you plan a trip to the Black Hills, don't forget to get your picture taken in front of Mount Rushmore!

Visitors walk along the Avenue of Flags toward Mount Rushmore.

Glossary

cathedral (kuh-THEE-drull) A cathedral is a large church. Gutzon Borglum carved sculptures in a cathedral.

dynamite (DUY-nuh-myte) Dynamite is an explosive that can be used to break things apart. Gutzon Borglum used dynamite to carve Mount Rushmore.

Emancipation Proclamation (ee-man-sih-PAY-shun prok-luh-MAY-shun) The Emancipation Proclamation was an 1863 order given by President Lincoln to free the slaves.

granite (GRAN-it) Granite is a type of very hard rock. Mount Rushmore is made of light-colored granite.

Great Depression (GRAYT dee-PRESH-un) The Great Depression was a period of time in the 1930s when many Americans couldn't find jobs. Mount Rushmore was built during the Great Depression.

model (MOD-ull) A model is a small copy of something. Models are sometimes used to plan sculptures.

monument (MON-yoo-munt) A monument is something made in memory of an important person or event. Mount Rushmore is a monument.

peak (PEEK) A peak is the top of a mountain. Mount Rushmore's peak is 6,000 feet (1,829 meters) high.

sculptor (SKULP-tur) A sculptor is an artist who carves statues. Gutzon Borglum was a sculptor.

sketches (SKECH-ez) Sketches are simple drawings. Sketches were used to plan the faces on Mount Rushmore.

studio (STOO-dee-oh) A place where artists do their work is a studio. Gutzon Borglum's studio is at Mount Rushmore.

Find Out More

IN THE LIBRARY

Coury, Tina Nichols, and Sally Wern Comport (illustrator). *Hanging Off Jefferson's Nose: Growing Up On Mount Rushmore.* New York: Dial Books for Young Readers, 2012.

Patrick, Jean L.S., Mary Anne Maier, and Patrick Faricy (illustrator). *Face to Face with Mount Rushmore.* Keystone, SD: Mount Rushmore History Association, 2008.

Thomas, William David. *Mount Rushmore.* New York: Chelsea Clubhouse, 2010.

ON THE WEB

Visit our Web site for lots of links about Mount Rushmore:
www.childsworld.com/links

Note to Parents, Teachers, and Librarians: We routinely check our Web links to make
sure they're safe, active sites—so encourage your readers to check them out!

Index